Who Are African Americans?

AA Cultural Literacy
Publications

To Yash, Seth, Michael & Amari

Published in 2024 by
AA Cultural Literacy Publications
P.O. Box 3190
McDonough, GA 30253

ISBN: 979-8-218-97933-1
Printed in the USA

Edited & designed by Nekeyba

Contents

Introduction ...4

What's in a name? ...7

What is an "ethnic group"? ...8

Who are African Americans? ...10

How did African Americans get the name "African American"? ...14

Foundational Black Americans ...18

How African Americans made the US a better place ...20

Freedom, Opportunity & Democracy ...32

In Conclusion ...38

Why learn about African American history? ...40

Learn More/ Resources ...42

Glossary ...50

Introduction

TEA-ASK™ stands for *Things Every African-American Should Know.* **TEA-ASK**™ is an *African American Cultural Literacy (AACL)* resource designed to answer the parent, guardian, teacher and student who desires to learn more about *African American* people.

TEA-ASK *Family Share* books are written for children. We encourage children and their adult family members to read these books together.

5

What's In A Name?

Have you ever wondered how people or groups of people get their names? Like why are African Americans *called **African Americans**?*

Well, there are lots of ways that a group of people or an ***ethnic group*** gets its name. The most common way is from the place where a person lives or was born. Like a person who lives in *Jamaica* would be called "Jamaican." A person from *Nigeria* is called "Nigerian." A person living in *Puerto Rico* is "Puerto Rican."

These people may travel or move to another country, but still may be called the name of their home land or *ethnic group.*

What is an "ethnic group"?

An **ethnic group** is a group of people who have some important things in common. Members of an *ethnic group* come from the same place and share a similar background and history. They share the same language, culture and traditions. *Korean, Italian, Irish, Haitian,* and *Cherokee* are all examples of ethnic groups.

African Americans are also an *ethnic group*! They have had different names over the years. However, they are still the same people who share the same history, language, culture and traditions.

Who Are the African Americans?

African Americans are people whose ancestors were taken from countries in West Africa to work as slaves in the United States a long time ago. Some of those African countries are *Angola, Senegal, Gambia, Ghana, Nigeria* and *the Congo.*

African people were brought to places in North America, South America, the Caribbean and Europe. **The African people who were brought to the United States became African Americans.**

These Africans were first brought to Virginia in **1619.** Their families have lived in many parts of the United States ever since then.

African Americans are an *ethnic group* that is a mixture of West African, some Native American and some European peoples. Some have very little or no mixture in their **genes**.

However, what makes them "African American" is their ancestry, their unique history, their traditions and their culture.

13

How did African Americans get the name, "African American"?

There were names that people used for African people when they came to the shores of America. Two of those names were "African" and "Colored."

In the late 1800s, Booker T. Washington* thought it was a good idea for them to call themselves "Negro." He thought it would help the Africans in America to be more united. *Negro* was the name for *African American* people for a long time.

***Booker T. Washington** was a teacher, a speaker and a very important leader. He started *Tuskegee University* in 1881. He believed *African American* people should work hard and develop skills to make their lives better. 15

During the **Civil Rights Movement** in the 1950s and 1960s, many **Negros** started using the word "Black" instead of *Negro*. This helped to unify the different Black ethnic groups that later came to the United States.

Some also used the name "Afro-American" because it made them proud of their African heritage. That name helped *African Americans* feel more confident about who they are and where they came from.

Today, the two most common names for *African American people* are: "African American" and "Black American."

Foundational Black Americans

Foundational Black Americans (**FBA**) is another name that you might start hearing more and more. Some people use this name because it identifies the Black people who were in the United States for a very long time.

American Descendants of Slavery or **ADOS** is another name that you may hear. This name is used for a movement that wants fairness for the Black people who were forced to work as slaves in the United States.

Both **FBA** and **ADOS** are names for *African American* people. These names help to better identify them as a unique group.

African Americans are a special group of people who have done a lot to build the United States and make it a better place!

How African Americans Made the United States A Better Place

A long time ago, *African Americans* were made to work without getting paid. They were **enslaved** and were treated as **slaves** for a long time.

During *slavery*, *FBAs* built many things. They built roads and railroads used for traveling. They built other important structures too, like *the White House, the U.S. Capitol building* and several universities.

During those years, *African Americans* also grew raw materials and produced lots of products. They picked lots of cotton, rice, tobacco and sugar. These and other crops were used to make money for some families and for the United States government.

Sadly, all of this happened when *African Americans* were forced to be *slaves.* When they were enslaved, *FBAs* were treated like property and didn't get any of the money they helped make.

The money made from African American slave labor helped the United States become a wealthy nation.

24

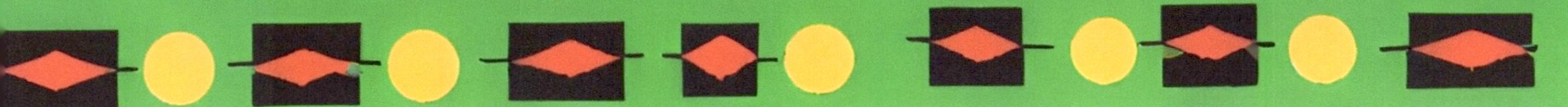

African American Soldiers. . .

Throughout U.S. history, *African Americans* have been brave **soldiers** in every war! *African American* soldiers fought in big wars like *the American Revolution, the Civil War, the Vietnam War*, and *the Gulf wars*. The United States won many battles because of the help of many, many fearless *African American* men and women soldiers.

But that's not all!

ADOS have done so much to influence American science, politics, sports, entertainment, education and the arts.

African Americans **invented** many important things like the pencil sharpener, the gas mask, and folding chairs. They created potato chips and mac and cheese. And they made fried chicken popular!

African Americans made important parts for computers and invented ways to do heart and eye surgery. Their inventions saved lives and helped many people. We can thank Otis Boykin, Vivien Thomas, and Patricia Bath for this.

In sports, *ADOS* have set many records. Wilt Chamberlain in basketball and Barry Bonds in baseball. *Joe Louis* still reigns as a boxing champ and Sha'Carri Richardson is now the fastest woman in the world!

African American Music. . .

Music is an area that *African Americans* have had a big impact. They have influenced music in the United States and music throughout the world!

African Americans created **the Blues** music. *Blues* is very important because many other popular music forms come from it.   *Hip-Hop/Rap*, *Pop*, *Rock*, *Country*, *Rhythm and Blues*, and *Jazz* can all be traced back to *the Blues*.

The Blues and other *African American* music forms have influenced many types of music all around the world.

Have you ever heard of *Reggae, Afrobeats, Techno or British Rock?* They have all been influenced by *African American* music!

Even some popular music from video games have been influenced by *FBA* music! Did you know that *Nintendo games* often use **Ragtime** music for their *Super Mario Bros* games? *Ragtime* is a type of piano music that was created a long time ago by *American Descendants of Slavery (ADOS).*

That's pretty cool, huh?

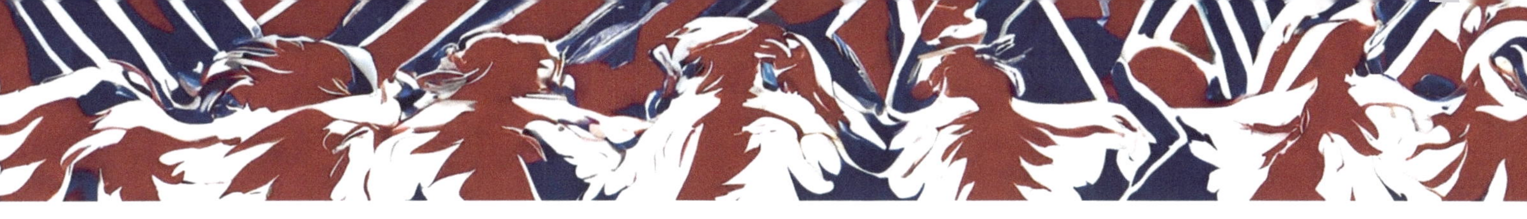

Music is very important. But there is something even more important that *African Americans* did and continue to do in the United States of America. . .

. . .

African Americans have helped the United States continue to grow as a nation of *Freedom, Opportunity and Democracy!*

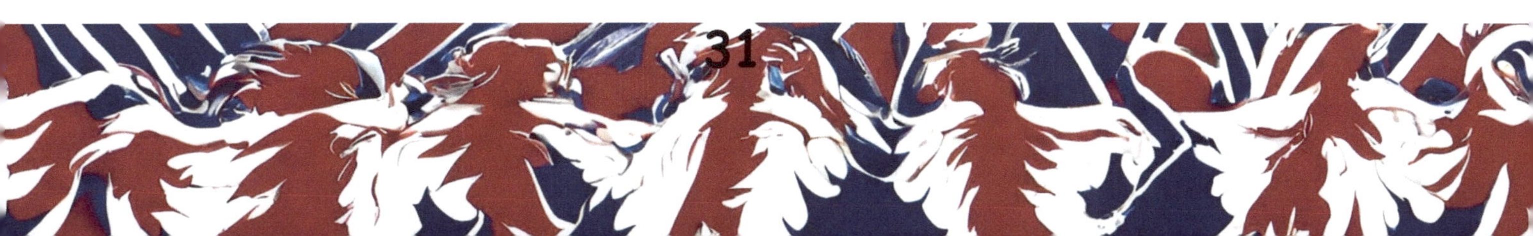

Freedom, Opportunity and Democracy

Most people think of **Freedom, Opportunity** and **Democracy** when they think of the United States. In this country, a person has the *freedom* to live according to their own choices.

In the U.S., children go to school for *free*. People have *opportunities* to buy homes and open businesses. A person might get the *opportunity* to use their talent, skill or creativity to become rich and famous. And citizens use *democracy* to make life better for everyone.

Many places in the world do not have this kind of *Freedom, Opportunity or Democracy.* Many places are not like the United States.

But the United States wasn't always like this. Many people, and especially *African Americans*, did not have equal rights or freedom. And they definitely could not vote!

However, during the **Civil Rights Movement**, many people fought to change unfair laws and policies. *Civil Rights* laws made it so that all citizens could vote and participate equally in society. *Civil Rights* allow people to work, live and go to school where they choose.

African Americans were the leaders in the *Civil Rights Movement*. They played a very big role in causing those unfair practices to be changed. As a result, the United States has become a better place to live for everyone.

African Americans helped make the United States a freer and more **democratic** place to live. Lots of people come to the United States because of that.

The U.S. is not perfect, but it is their land and their home. African Americans are United States **citizens**.

And as citizens, African Americans have the right to enjoy all of the good that the country has to offer. They must also help to make things better, just like they have always done in the United States!

In Conclusion. . .

So, who are the African American people?

African Americans (FBA and ADOS) are an ethnic group of people whose great-great-great grandparents were taken from countries in West Africa. They were brought to the United States to work as slaves, but they never stopped fighting for their freedom! Along the way, they have shared their many gifts and talents with the U.S. And by fighting for freedom, they help make the U.S. a freer and more democratic place to live for everyone.

The United States of America is a better place because of African American people!

Why Learn About *African American* History?

African American history IS American history!

As you learn more about *African American* people, you are learning more about the history of this great nation called the United States.

Reread this book and share it with others. Read other books in the **TEA-ASK™** and **TEA-ASK Family Share series** to learn more about this unique and special group of people. . .the *African American* people.

Learn More. . .

There are many places where you can go to learn more. There are national and even international sites that honor the *African American* people or individual *African Americans.*   Nearly every state in the United States has museums, historic sites and monuments dedicated to the lives and work of the *African American* people.

Included is a short list of historic sites and museums. Visit these sites in person with family and friends! Or go to their websites to learn more about the rich history of *African Americans.*

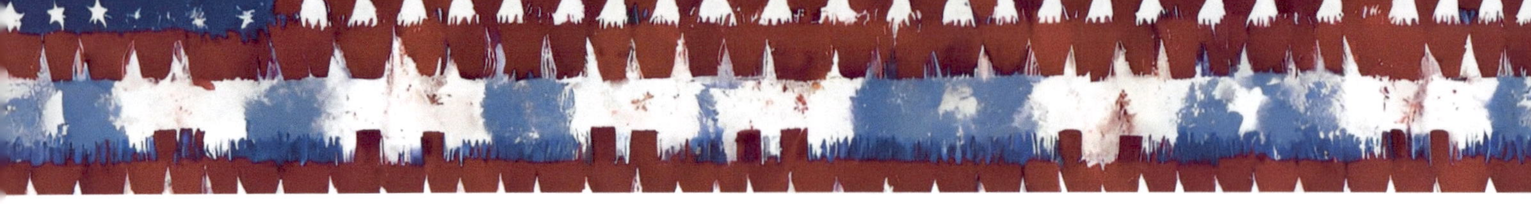

General Museums

- National Museum of African American History and Culture - Washington, DC
- Museum of African American History - Boston, MA
- California African American Museum - Los Angeles, CA
- Apex Museum - Atlanta, GA
- DuSable Museum of African American History - Chicago, IL
- International African American Museum - Charleston, SC
- Schomburg Center for Research in Black Culture - New York, NY
- Charles H. Wright Museum of African American History - Detroit, MI

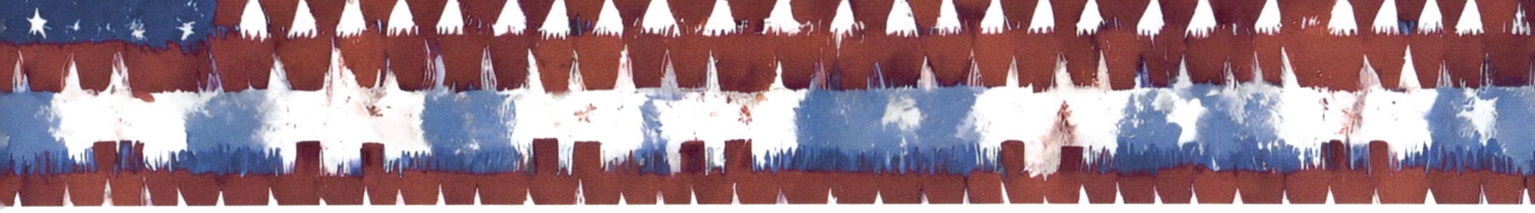

Civil & Human Rights

- National Civil Rights Museum - Memphis, TN
- National Center for Civil and Human Rights - Atlanta, GA
- National Voting Rights Museum and Institute - Selma, AL
- National Underground Railroad Freedom Center - Cincinnati, OH
- Underground Railroad Heritage Center - Niagara Falls, NY

African American Heroes/Sheroes

- National Great Blacks in Wax Museum - Baltimore, MD
- George Washington Carver National Monument -
   Diamond, MO
- Martin Luther King Historic District - Atlanta, GA
- Madame C.J. Walker Boutique Museum - Atlanta, GA
- Jackie Robinson Museum - New York, NY
- The Mary McLeod Bethune Home - Daytona Beach, FL

Sports and Entertainment

- National Museum of African American Music -
   Nashville, TN
- Rock and Roll Hall of Fame - Cleveland, OH
- New Orleans Jazz Museum - New Orleans, LA
- Negro Leagues Baseball Museum - Kansas City, MO

Memorials, Historic Sites & Landmarks

- Brown v. Board of Education National Historic Site - Topeka, KS
- New Orleans National Historic Park - New Orleans, LA
- Whitney Plantation - Edgard, LA
- Harriet Tubman Underground Railroad National Historical Park - Church Creek, MD
- Shabazz Memorial and Educational Center - New York, NY
- African American Civil War Memorial - Washington, DC
- Pullman National Monument - Chicago, IL
- United Nations Slavery Memorial, "the Ark of Return" - UN, NYC
- Savannah Black History Tour - Savannah, GA

Military & War

- Tuskegee Airmen National Historic Site - Tuskegee, AL
- African American Military History Museum - Hattiesburg, MS
- African American Civil War Museum - Washington, DC
- Buffalo Soldiers National Museum - Houston, TX
- Buffalo Soldiers Memorial Park - Fort Leavenworth, KS
- Port Chicago Naval Magazine National Memorial Park - Concord, CA

Glossary

Genes are tiny parts inside your body that decide things like your hair type, eye color, nose shape and how tall you are. You get your genes from your parents.

Civil Rights are the basic rights that everyone should have, like being treated fairly and being able to go to the same schools and places as everyone else.

Civil Rights Movement was a time during the 1950s and 1960s when people worked together to make sure everyone, especially African Americans, was treated fairly and had the same rights.

FBA stands for *Foundational Black American*

ADOS stands for *American Descendants of Slavery*

Invent means to make something new that nobody has made before.

Democratic means that everyone gets to have a say in making decisions, like voting for what they want.

Ragtime is a type of piano music that has a fun, bouncy rhythm and was popular in the early 1900s. Ragtime music was created by African Americans.

The Blues is a type of music that tells stories about feelings, like being sad or happy, and has a special, soulful sound. Many other music styles like Rock & Roll, Jazz, and Hip-Hop came from the Blues. The Blues was created by African Americans.